NEVER ENDING LOVE

BY GEORGE GUTHRIE

PAGE PUBLISHING
Conneaut Lake, PA

First originally published by Page Publishing 2024

ISBN 979-8-89157-333-8 (pbk)
ISBN 979-8-89157-350-5 (digital)

Printed in the United States of America

Contents

The Essence of Love

You're like a light that brightens my dark path,
I find strength in your smile.
Being around you is a breath of fresh air,
When I'm with you my heart skips a beat.
I can't help but to stare,
Just seeing you my face becomes flush with heat.
Your beauty is like nothing I've seen before,
When I am in your presence I don't feel alone.
My worries evaporate when I am beside you,
Now, I know what it is like to be in the presence of an angel.
I will do whatever it takes to be by your side,
I will deal with any challenges that come our way.
I pray that one day you will stay,
Your voice is as sweet as honey.
I could hear your voice all day and never get tired,
Your smile could stop any man in his tracks.
And it could tame even the wildest beast,
I will follow you to the moon if that what it takes.
Without you, I am like a fish out of water,
Or a tree without dirt.

Lucky Me

I have to be the luckiest man I know,
I found this woman who smiles even when she is on the go.
She never puts on a show,
Maybe that is why people flock to her and not just because of her
natural glow.
I have never seen her flaunt when she is out,
This is a sexy, strong, independent black woman. No doubt.
This woman talks to people even when others have turned into
a shout,
She stays calm throughout the bout.
As I look back, I notice how different we are in our ways,
You stay calm and collective; Mine are spontaneous and may change
depending on the day.
Since we both like to play,
There is only one thing to say.
I pray that we will meet again someday,
But, right now, I must be on my way.

A Day of Depression

As I lay here counting sheep,
I am hoping that it will help me go to sleep.
   Sleep falls upon me so late into the night,
That here it is almost daylight.
   When I woke up, I felt like I had gotten into a fight,
My face was all puffy and red; I looked quite a sight.
   I feel worse now than when I went to bed,
My body feels as heavy as lead, and my mind can't grasp what you
   just said.
   As I called my work to request some time off,
I lied when I said that I had a bad cough.
   I couldn't bring myself to tell people that my depression had
   gotten worse,
It is like I am dealing with a bad curse.
   This illness I cannot shake away,
I have falling and become its prey.
   My meds have helped the symptoms stay at bay,
However, this illness will be with me till my dying day.

Without You

Without you my life is incomplete,
I feel like a man who is facing defeat.
My days are lonely without you by my side,
All I want to do is hide; Without you being here, it feels as though I
have died.
I think of you every single day,
And wish that you were here beside me, instead of being so far away.
I want us to be together in everything we do,
Only you can turn my gray days blue.
I miss your soft touch, and the sound of your voice drives me
crazy,
I think just maybe, that I have fallen over heels for you, my lady.
This loneliness and sadness that I feel when I am away from you
is no fake,
From this nightmare of being without you, I wish I would awake.
My love for you is not something that I want to shake,
However, without you by my side, I feel like I am in the middle of a
category 10 earthquake.

Lover's Lane

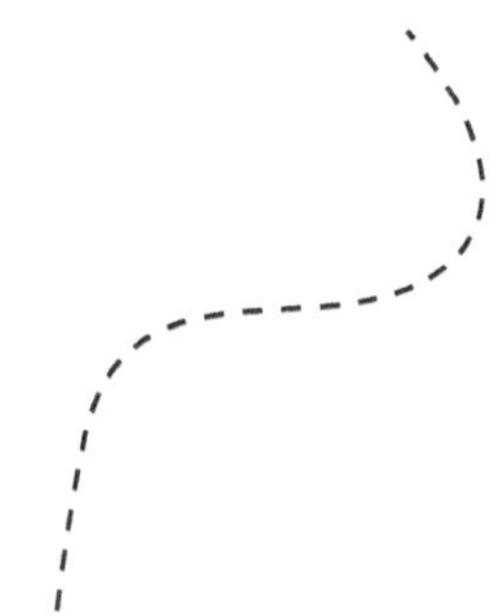

Our love and feelings for one another is so exquisite; it is as if
we have found the holy grail,
We should both settle down and stop chasing tail.
We should know one another so well,
And things should be as smooth as a blind man reading brail.
My love for you runs so deep and is so strong,
That these days and nights without you seem wrong and are way,
way, too long.
Every day that passes that you are not here with me,
It is another day of depression and pain. It is as if I have run headfirst
into a tree.
You are one of the most magnificent, intelligent, and the most
beautiful woman I know,
I wish that I could stay with you and never let you go.

Addicted to You

I will go the extra mile,
Just to see you smile.
I want to brighten up your day,
And make that frown of yours go away.
I know that I have made you sad,
However, I want to show you that I can make you happy and glad.
I am lost without you by my side,
It hurts so much that it feels as though I have died.
Only to be awakened by your presence and the sound of your voice,
This just reassured me that I had made the right choice.
My heart and mind have been aching since you have not been here,
Every day that passes I feel more and more fear;
It is like I am losing you, my dear.
I dream of having you in my arms and holding you tight,
I hope that one day we will be together again. Maybe then things will be alright.

Lovestruck

If pain was love,
Then I would be flying overhead like a dove.
You and I fit together like a glove,
Therefore, we should keep praying to the man up above.
Our love grows stronger each and every day,
But together, we will overcome whatever that is in our way.
We may gain more and more haters every passing day,
So let us not falter; for together we must stay.
You are like the sun that lights up my path,
I want you like people need water to take a bath.
Sometimes we might fight,
Nevertheless, we always try to settle them before we say good night.
I have been swept off my feet,
By your kisses that are so sweet.
My face has turned as red as a beet,
The cause of it is you, not this heat.
Every time that you are around,
My heart starts to pound like an earthquake in the ground.
You are like a diamond that has not been found,
I can't wait! I am now homeward bound.

Flaming Emotions

You say our love is true, yet you are blue,
You have blamed me for the things that I did and didn't do.
You have used every excuse in the book to justify your actions,
Nevertheless, you want your words to cause satisfaction.
You talk like you have given up on us,
And you say things, knowing that it will cause a fuss.
Since you do not know what is at store,
You run for the door and over time you start running more and more.
No matter where you go, people will get into our affairs. But who cares?
There will always be somebody looking upon us with a stare,
The only way that we can overcome it is if we stay a pair.
You and I should dwell on things that matter,
And not indulge in this useless chatter.
Why do we let these things ruin our day?
Even though we are both guilty of believing what people say.
I know that things are hard for you to deal with right now,
However, we should try to make it even though we don't know how.
Physically, we might not be together but for a few hours each week,
But, with every hour that passes, it is you that I seek.
My heart and mind aches when you are not by my side,
These tears are for you, so hang on and be satisfied.

Feeling without Shame

Times are rough right now, I know,
Yet, hold on tight; maybe then our love will grow.
All this time away from you has made my heart cry out in pain,
I love you so much that tears fall from my eyes like rain.
There has never been anybody that has made me feel this way,
But, being without you, even my sunniest days seem gloomy and
gray.
Once I become united with you, that is when the sun will come
out again:
I can take my troubles like a fist to the chin,
But, what I can't take is not being able to see your dimples when you
grin.

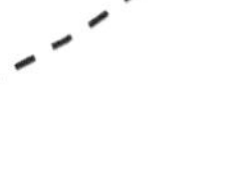

The Essence of Destruction

At times you make me want to cut my losses and start over,
Yet, here I stand, refusing to give up on us or run for cover.
I stay knowing the consequences,
Only for you do I let down my defenses.
If I have hurt you, it was not done intentionally,
It was not done out of anger or hate; so stop making things bigger emotionally.
People will try to test us in every way,
It is up to us to fall prey or to carry on about our day.
You have pushed me away more time than I can say,
Even when I should have run as far as I could, I stayed.
Sooner or later, you are going to push so hard that I will be gone,
Maybe then you will realize that I was not so wrong.

Endless Love

As I lay here wishing you were here beside me,
I have become captured by your love, and I don't want to break free.
I cherish all the time we have spent together,
Regardless of how stormy the weather.
Without you beside me I feel desolate,
You are the only one who can make me feel consummate.
I have made it known that I love you,
Cupid's dart has hit his mark; without you, I don't know what to do.
My heart becomes broken every time you leave,
But, best believe, it is for you that I grieve.
You are the only one who has ever made me stumble over my
words and go weak in the knees,
There is nobody who can take your place; only you do I please.
I will go to the extreme to make sure that you are happy and
satisfied,
You know my past, so there will be nothing to hide. All I want is you
by my side.

No Remorse

It feels as though my feelings for you is not mutual,
I hear you proclaiming that you love me, but it is not truthful.
What's in your heart should show,
No excuses. Some things you should already know.
We are nine months into this relationship,
Yet, you don't trust me, and you always give me lip.
I am not a hard man to please,
But best believe, right now, I am not at ease.
You have warned my patience thin,
We are supposed to be a couple. But instead, we are fighting like we
are full of gin.
I still want you beside me, no matter what I do,
However, the choice is yours whether I go on with or without you.

Dreams Come True

These days seem way too cold without having you to hold,
You are more precious to me than diamonds are gold.
Every time that I look around, I am reminded of you,
I want you beside me, no matter what I do.
Through all these years of fighting and bitchin',
I never thought to sit back and listen, until I was crying over what I
was missin'.
It was you. Baby. You are the one that I have been looking for
all along,
I have fallen head over heels in love with you. Now I am beating on
my chest like King Kong.
I hope that one day we can seal this deal,
That way all my dreams will come real.

Alone

Your presence alone makes me smile,
Like a child that hasn't seen his mother in a while.
By you saying goodbye, it has broken my heart into little pieces,
I will never forget how you have helped me stay as sharp as creases.
Nothing is going to be the same after you leave,
You best believe, it is going to be even harder to brush these haters
off my sleeve.
You come one in a million, not a dime a dozen,
When you are here, you give off this vibe that has everybody buzzin'.
I have to give credit where credit is due,
Your showed compassion and with it my willingness grew.
You have helped people with your eagerness and your listening
ear,
With you beside me, I have overcome some of my darkest fears.
It's a thought you already know what is needed to help me,
And you have done this with such grace that I feel free.
Every day you are up-tempo and treat others like they are grown,
Who knew that one day you would say goodbye to your second
home?
We are like a family that is losing one of their own,
Now, I have to go back to being alone.
It is hard losing someone who is so special;
I will never forget the way that you have treated others,
You treated me not only like a brother but also like a lover.

Looking Back

You play with my emotions more than wheels at a state fair,
You have slung lies around like nobody is going to care.
It should be obvious why my temper is flaring,
Even when things become overbearing. We still are not sharing.
We have started to fight more,
Everything we do strikes us to the core;
Now we are both running for the door.
We have made excuses of why things didn't work,
We have failed to see what was in front of us all along;
I will be the first to admit that I was a total jerk.
We fault with each other, not looking for an understanding. Yet,
we expected one all the same,
Neither one of us wanted to hurt the other with our demands.
We crossed paths while we were going our separate ways,
Know, I just hope that this is not another phase.

The Best Thing That Happened

Spending this time without you,
Has only made me want you more;
Since you have been gone, my days have turned gray instead of blue.
Seeing your smiling face and your beauty,
Melts my worries away;
I want to be yours truly, and never go astray.
You are like the day to my night,
I am your prince who will never leave your side;
I want to hold you tight, with nothing to hide.
You uplift everybody that you come into contact with,
We fit together like biscuits and gravy, and that's no myth.
I want to be by your side when you are hurting or in pain,
I hope that you know that I am for real, with no games.
When I am away from you, my heart grows heavy as a chain,
But with you I have no shame.
Without you I've lost my better half,
But when I am around you, I am as happy as a cow that has found
its calf.
With you, I am complete like milk is to cake,
I want to hold you in my arms and make you laugh;
I will do whatever it takes.

Thinking of You

It is what's on the inside that counts,
What's on the outside is just a bonus;
So there is no need to get mad and bounce.
Let's sit down and talk this out,
Maybe then we can find out why this has come about.
It is nothing like a conversation to get things straight,
Maybe then we can clear the slate;
If only we could congratulate one another instead of hate.
Before one of us jumps to any conclusion,
We must look within ourself for a solution.
We must stay real with ourself,
Then we want have to worry if we are turning left.

One's Helpful Ways

At times I can't find my way,
But when I see you, everything seems okay.
You have made an impact on everyone you meet,
But that is not the only thing that makes you unique.
You must have been sent from up above,
Maybe that is why people show you love.
You are an angel in disguise,
Some might despise;
But to me, you are the prize.
I see how you treat others,
You treat them like they are your sisters and brothers.
Very few people show others respect,
And that can lead to people doing things that they will regret;
Yet, sometimes that is what we forget.

Princess to Be

Your love is like a magnet that draws me near,
Don't fear, your prince charming is here.
Nothing will keep me from being by your side,
So there is no reason to hide.
As I admire this beauty before me,
My heart starts beating so fast, it feels like it's trying to break free.
My love for you grows stronger each and every day,
So just stay and not run away.
This prince wants you as his princess if you will accept it,
Just know that my love will never quit.
I want to hold you in my arms day and night,
I will never let you go, not without a fight.

Changing Places

> Things are happening way too fast,
> There's no present, just the past.
> My mind has become a grenade,
> It does not wound; it kills like raid.
> Stop kidding yourself if you think that I am going to fade,
> I am going to loom over you, more than the shade.
> You have talked negatively about me, like I'm some kind of disease,
> Yet, you want me to say please;
> While you sit on your high horse eating cheese.
> You have looked down your nose, like I am beneath you,
> However, when everything was said and done, you stood there like you were in glue.
> Now that the birds have fled the coop,
> And you don't have your group;
> You have found yourself outside the loop.
> Who knew that you would become the same as I?
> The very one whom you have despised;
> Is now the very one you have to depend on to live or die.
> Whether we sigh or cry,
> At the end of the day, we both have to get by.

Never-Ending Love

We are two lonely hearts that have found one another,
We fit together as if one of us was the bread, and the other was the
butter.
Your beauty makes my heart skip a beat,
I have fallen in love with you. What a treat!
When we are together, the sun always shines,
However, when you are away, my heart grows heavy like I am carry-
ing a pine.
This love that we share is one of a kind,
You have captured not only my heart but my mind.
I have been struck by cupid's dart,
Our love has become so strong that nothing can break us apart.
It has been five years since we have met,
Now with all the wedding plans, we are set.

Standing Tall

I find myself captured by your glow,
I want everybody to know.
 That I am lovestruck, and I don't care that it shows,
For you I will fight, no matter where we go.
 I do believe that we make a good couple,
I am going to have to fight other men because I have found my dia-
 mond in the rubble.
 You shine brighter than any stone that I have ever saw,
I have to admit; in you, I can't find a flaw.
 I would put you and your kids before any other,
I want you. And only you, as my friend, companion, and lover.
 I have found where I belong. That is with you.
I just hope that you can say the same;
That way we can be together, no matter what we do.

No Other

I want our love to get better like aged wine,
I will never leave you behind;
Maybe this is our sign.
	I am jotting down a few lines,
To show you that you are on my mind.
	Who knew what we were going to find?
Once our hearts embrace, and we become entwined.
	Every time we get together, it is mind-blowing,
And our love starts growing.
	Now I have my queen to hold,
I would not trade her for anything. Not even a pot of gold.
	Just one look is all it took,
Now you have me hooked.

Straightforward

It takes everything that I have not to wrap my arms around you,
    and put my lips on yours,
When I see you, my heart doesn't just leap for joy, it soars.
    I guess time will tell how well we fit together,
Who knew that we would make each other better?
    I want you to be beside me in all that I do,
There is no one else. Only you.
    I hope that you are not with someone else when I am not there,
Because I do not like to share.
    I am not a jealous man,
But do not push it.
    I will be beside you like your number one fan,
And I will fight for you, like two dogs in a pit.

Spoken from the Heart

With all your excuses, I am now in an emotional whirlwind,
For you though, this is just a trend.
You have put me through every emotion and then some,
You have played me like I am dumb.
At times, you make me so mad that I want to leave,
Yet, I stay because I love you, without any tricks up my sleeve.
Why must we argue when there is no need to do so?
Are you doing this just for a show?
Maybe you should just let things go,
Then in turn our love will grow.
If you keep holding on to what people say and things of the
past,
Then one thing is for sure, our love will not last.
Just like the sky can be overcast,
You can lose me just as fast.
I am not saying these things to break your heart,
However, I am telling you these things in hopes that we will stay
together and not drift apart.

Reminiscing

Your kisses are as sweet as candy,
All it takes is one touch from you, and my body goes crazy.
You have dreads the color of gold,
There is nobody in this world that I would rather hold.
When you smile, it brightens up my day,
I wonder if that twinkle in your eye is here to stay.
Your skin feels soft and smooth under my touch,
You are the only one that I want for breakfast, supper, and lunch.
Now that we are together, I never want to leave,
All we have to do is believe.
When you laugh, it is like music to my ears,
However, when I am without you, my eyes become wet with tears.

Seeing Things through My Eyes

Living in the days past,
Thought that we would always last.
Who knew that our relationship would end so fast?
Only we can stop what our shadow has cast.
This has gone on too long without some understanding,
I know that I am rough around the edges and in need of some sanding.
I understand that I fly off without a landing,
But, who knew that one day I would be a victim of my own mishandling?
For years I have lived by survival instincts, without anybody by my side,
Then you came along, and I felt like I had nothing to hide.
It felt like you were with me, not just for the ride,
Once again, I was left with a broken heart that feels like I had died.
Even through all your cheating, I never lied,
On the outside I became angry, but on the inside I cried.
I stood by you, no matter what choices you made,
Yet, this is how I get repaid.
People have fed you lies, like they are playing charade,
Now they just sit back and gloat, like they got an A as a grade.

Only You

Every day that passes, I fall more in love with you,
I never thought that I would find someone that would make me feel
    the way you do.
    You make my head spin and my heart skip a beat,
If it wasn't for you, I would be facing defeat.
    Holding you in my arms and being near you seems so right,
I want you to stay with me every night.
    The times that I am away from you, I feel lonely and sad,
I count the minutes, hours, and days until I can be united with you;
You are the best thing that I ever had.
    There is not a day or night that you are not on my mind,
No matter what I do and where I go, I will not leave you behind.
    I am very lucky to have someone so special by my side,
I am happy that I found you, and we do not have to hide;
You have turned my dreams into a reality.

Nothing to Hide

I proclaim my love for you,
However, it seems as though you don't have a clue about loving me
too.
The more words I speak and the more actions that I show,
You! You throw it, all of it, out the window.
I am smarter than you think I am,
Yet, you treat me like I am some artificial lame.
Why must you stab me in the back when I am not around?
This is not how we find solid ground;
If anything, this will make our love drown.
I am tired of playing mister nice guy,
With a person like you who doesn't even want to try.
I am hipped to your lie,
But, the same thing that makes you laugh can also make you cry.
One way or another, I am going to find out the truth,
And it is not going to come from some gypsy fortune-telling booth.
I did not fall head over heels because of some material things,
I fell in love with you, not knowing what it brings.
Real love will break down any wall of deception and will con-
quer all,
But, you have to be willing to stand tall and get up when you fall.

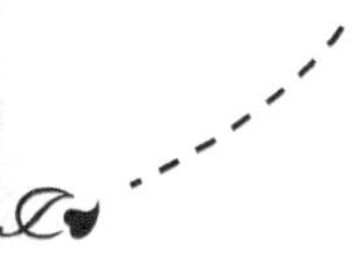

Struggle

You want me to watch my tone,
Yet, you are grinding bone against bone.
You leave without even calling my phone,
You say that I have hurt you;
But my ribs feel like they have been hit with a stone.
My actions were done out of reflex, not out of impulse,
You have taken my actions as some kind of insults.
Even though you wouldn't let me explain,
It seemed to cause more pain.
I bent over back words to help you understand,
But, I seem to be sinking faster, like standing in quicksand.
You make it seem as though I am not your boyfriend,
But a child who has to raise his hand.
You have made it perfectly clear of what you want and what you
are doing this for,
Instead of trying to make things work, you're throwing in the towel
and running for the door.
What you can't see is that you are not the only one sore,
There is no reason to claim war, so why keep score?
We do not need to discuss things that we already know,
But, before we go toe to toe, we need to find a solution or we will
not grow.
Stop treating me like I am your foe,
Because I am not. I am a man who has been beside you, no matter
what you show.

Better Half

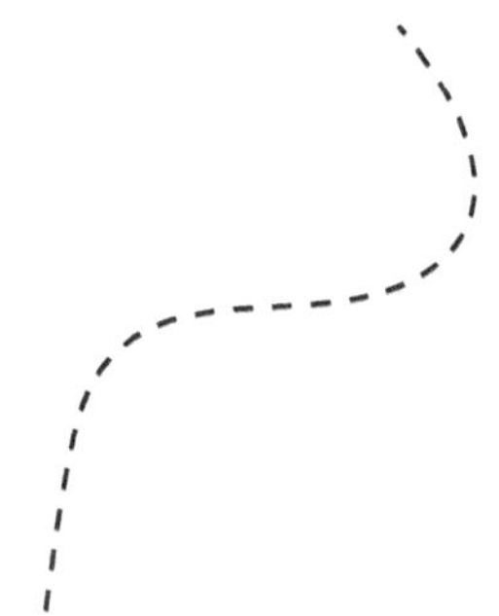

You make me feel like I am ten feet tall and can leap tall buildings in a single bound,
It is like I have been lost, but now I am found;
Without you, I am dead in the ground.
With you by myside, I feel victorious like a king winning a battle,
Who knew that we would fit together like a horse under a saddle?
I hope that this time apart does not change your feelings about us,
However, I do hope that it will make our bond stronger, and we can stop all this fuss.
I wish that I could shelter you from this stress and people's hateful ways,
But I can't. What I can do is love you and hold you till the end of my days.
When I am not around you, my stomach aches and twists into a ball,
I become like Humpty-Dumpty after he fell of the wall.
I know that so many times I have dropped the ball,
And that you get mad when I don't call.
But for you, I would beg and crawl,
I would rather love you than feel like a dead fly on the wall.

Faith, Love, and Happiness

I must have been dreaming,
Because I thought that you were beside me, with your face and eyes
gleaming.
Without having you to hold, I feel like a fish out of water,
When I think of you, my heart rate gets faster, and I get hot under
the collar.
I must have hit the lotto,
Because being with you, I feel whole instead of feeling hollow.
I wish that we had more time to spend together,
And spending a lifetime with you would be even better.
I want you beside me forever,
I would not leave your side again. Never!
I am not the same when you are not beside me,
But, all it takes is one look from you, and I light up like a Christmas
tree.
Through all our troubles, I hope that we can keep in touch,
I don't want to be a memory to you and seed through your mind, like
you have popped the clutch.

Yearning for More

I wish that you could stay with me,
Because being with you, I will feel free.
I know that at times, it seems as though I don't care,
But I do. I want us to be together as a pair.
You have captured not only my thoughts, but also my heart,
It is as if you were sent to me, so I could have a new start.
I want to be your lover, husband, and friend,
I want us to be there for each other till the end.
Let's both stop pretending like we are not in love with one another,
And hold fast to each other, no matter how stormy the weather.
I can't stop thinking about you,
I want you to be a part of everything that I do.
I want to try things that I have never tried before,
I hope that I am not coming off too strong and send you running for the door.
Baby, if you choose not to open up, then how are we going to find a solution?
There will always be away to settle our confusion and/or confrontations.

Unstable Relationship

I know that I messed up and sorry just won't cut it,
I have lost the best thing in my life because I did stupid shit.
I wish that I could change the hands of time,
And start over from when we first met, no rap no rhyme.
There is no excuse for my actions or words,
So I am not going to make any either;
But truth be told, my heart is aching like I have lost my bird.
The choice has always been yours, no matter who tries to influence you,
I have never misled you and have always told you the truth;
But can't you see that I'm hurting too?
This stress that I have been under these past few weeks has been the hardest thing mentally,
Because not once have I heard from you or been with you physically.
You might not want to hear this, but I love you with all my heart,
I hope that you will give us another shot before we depart.
I know that I have broken the bond that has bound us together,
Just maybe, we can salvage our relationship and pull through this stormy weather.

Never the Same

My heart has been hardened with frost,
That is not the only thing that has been lost.
　　You put me through hell, then you just up and ran,
Then you call to ask me to save you from another man.
　　You had me running around in circles so much that my eyes
　　have become crossed,
Now, I am losing what I have grossed.
　　I have become stressed because of the way you make me feel,
But, you have been running around telling others that it is me who
　　is making it such a big deal.
　　You have told so many lies that I don't know if what you say or
　　do is real,
I have cleaned things up, but there is no spill.
　　You keep throwing things in my face, like I owe you a bill,
You have me bouncing around so much that I can't sit still.
　　I find myself just going through the motions,
This conflict has become so natural it's like putting on lotion.
　　My words have fell on deaf ears, so it appears,
Now I am going to have to switch emotional gears;
And hopefully neither one of us will shed tears.

Mentally Challenging Love

You have me hooked, but I crave more,
I fear though that you will find somebody else and walk out the door.
We have grown to know each other quite well in a short time,
But what I feel for you can never fully be expressed in a rhyme.
We both have been hurt in the past,
So nobody except us should dictate how long we last.
As we live our own lives together, we should base everything on
respect, honesty, and trust,
Without these things, it is only lust;
And eventually our relationship will be a bust.
I want what we have to grow and prosper,
Not die and be disregarded like an old lobster.
I can't get you out of my brain,
Without you I cry out in pain, and it seems as though I'm going
insane.

Happiness Mixed with Sadness

As I sit here crying inside and wishing you would stay,
Who knew that your happiness would cause pain without going
away?
You have helped me in so many ways that there is no way that
I can repay,
You told me the truth when others kept me at bay.
You listened to my ramblings like it was a part of life,
But, who knew that your leaving would hurt worse than being cut
by a rusty old knife?
You are the closest family that one could hope for,
While you are smiling as you walk to the door;
People's mood start dropping to the floor.
Most of the time, you put a smile on everyone's face,
And when you are around, it is like nothing is out of place.
It is sometimes funny when people are fighting for your
attention,
You just laugh like it is something out of the movie Pulp Fiction.
I hope that you know that you will be missed when you leave
for your retirement,
I am going to try not to get sentimental, but I will in my own
confinement.

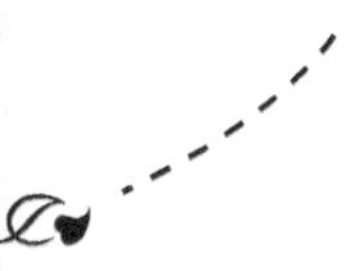

Digging You

Just like a rose can be blue,
I am sitting here, missing you.
    I let out a sigh,
Every time I see that twinkle in your eye.
    The sound of your voice makes my heart sing,
I am here to tell you that we are not just a fling.
    The sway of your body has me hooked in every way,
You have me hooked, line and sinker; I just can't stay away.

Finally at Peace

You're like the sun that brightens up my day,
You're the rain that washes all my pain away.
There is no place that I would rather be,
Than beside me, where I feel free.
Being away from you, my heart feels as heavy as lead,
And inside, I feel dead;
I can't stop these thoughts from racing through my head.
You have made me whole, like a light flashing into my soul,
Without you, my life has taken a down toll;
And I have become as dark as coal.
You have become my shining light that makes me strive for my
goal,
Without you, I just keep digging myself deeper into a hole.
As my love for you grows stronger,
I don't want to be alone any longer.
I have found my new home, and it's in your arms,
You have me chasing the rainbowlike lucky charms.
You have put a smile on my face like no other,
Every day you embrace me like a long-lost brother.
I want you with me for the rest of my life,
But only if you say yes as my wife.

Waiting for You

From the first day I met you,
I thought that my dreams come true.
I told you from the get-go,
That you will not have to change, but only if you want to.
Not once have I ever been a jealous person,
However, for you, there is always something lurking.
Instead of this being a prosperous relationship,
All you do is give me lip;
Which may cause me to jump from this liver's ship.
Every few weeks, we are at it again,
Sooner or later what we have will come to an end.
We will be worse off than when we began,
I will be like jumping out of the skillet into a waiting frying pan.
You have made it harder for me to find a common ground,
Yet, I stay because I am hoping that one day we will be happy and
homeward bound.

Love Conquers All

At one time, we were both traveling on a bumpy road,
Now that we have found each other, we have shed some of our heavy
load.
I cherish our relationship more than silver or gold,
As long as I have you to hold, I will never be cold.
At times, I would like to shed a tear,
But, knowing that you are by my side conquers my darkest fear.
Our hearts beat for each other like oldies that were before their
time,
We are like aged wine, and our love has found a place to dine.
I don't know how I would have made it without your caring-
ness, with your creativity thrown in,
I am your yang, and you are my yin.
When I am around such beauty, I become engulfed in happi-
ness, and I have to grin,
I get drunk off your love, like I drank a gallon of gin.

Holding Nothing Back

I don't want our relationship to be based on sex,
No reflex and no deleting each other like a text.
We should have an open communication,
Respect, trust, and be faithful to one another.
I want us to prosper,
Neither one of us should feel like we are face down in the gutter.
I know that we are going to have some ups and downs,
And we will probably run things into the ground.
But, at least at night,
We can hold on to one another and sleep tight.

All about You

As the sun dries up all the rain,
Your love washes away all my pain.
My love for you runs so deep,
That I think about you even when I am asleep.
I am drawn closer and closer to you each day,
No matter what, I am here to stay.
My feelings for you comes from within,
I am going to stay around like a piece of tin.
I want the whole world to see,
That you, and only you, can occupy this space beside me.
There is no place that I would rather be,
I want to hold you in my arms like a nest in a tree.

About the Author

The author was born in Eudora, Arkansas. The author traveled a lot. By going through foster care and D. H. S., he learned to take care of others. He grew up in an abusive, unstable, and strict environment. The author enjoys fishing, gardening, helping others, and listening to music.